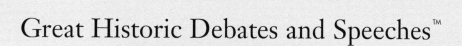

Great Historic Debates and Speeches™

SOJOURNER TRUTH'S "AIN'T I A WOMAN?" SPEECH

A PRIMARY SOURCE INVESTIGATION

Corona Brezina

rosen central
Primary Source™

The Rosen Publishing Group, Inc., New York

Published in 2005 by The Rosen Publishing Group, Inc.
29 East 21st Street, New York, NY 10010

Copyright © 2005 by The Rosen Publishing Group, Inc.

First Edition

Unless otherwise attributed, all quotes in this book are excerpted from Frances Gage's account of Sojourner Truth's "Ain't I a woman?" speech.

Library of Congress Cataloging-in-Publication Data

Brezina, Corona.
Sojourner Truth's "Ain't I a woman?" speech: a primary source investigation / by Corona Brezina.— 1st ed.
    p. cm. — (Great historic debates and speeches)
ISBN 1-4042-0154-8
1. Truth, Sojourner, d. 1883—Juvenile literature. 2. African American abolitionists—Biography—Juvenile literature. 3. Abolitionists—United States—Biography—Juvenile literature. 4. African American women—Biography—Juvenile literature. 5. Social reformers—United States—Biography—Juvenile literature. 6. Truth, Sojourner, d. 1883—Oratory—Juvenile literature. 7. Speeches, addresses, etc., American—African American authors—History and criticism—Juvenile literature. 8. Speeches, addresses, etc., American—Women authors—History and criticism—Juvenile literature.
I. Title. II. Series.
E185.97.T8B74 2005
306.3'62'092—dc22

                                                                    2004001443

Manufactured in the United States of America

Cover images: Left: Undated hand-colored portrait of Sojourner Truth. Right: An illustration depicting an 1880 women's rights convention in Chicago, Illinois.

CONTENTS

Sojourner Truth is one of the most legendary reformers in American history. She was one of the major advocates for abolition and women's rights during the nineteenth century. She sold copies of this undated portrait of herself and of her autobiography during her many lecture tours.

This engraving portrays delegates at a women's rights convention during the late nineteenth century. Sojourner Truth participated in several of these forums.

INTRODUCTION

On May 29, 1851, an illiterate ex-slave named Sojourner Truth attended a women's rights convention in Akron, Ohio. She was tall with striking features and had a voice that was once described as the sound of thunderclaps. As the convention's only black participant, she stood out among the sea of white faces in attendance. But what she had to say was even more outstanding. It was here that Sojourner Truth gave her "Ain't I a woman?" speech, one of the landmark speeches in American history.

Speaking in folksy English with a Dutch accent, Sojourner captured her audience's attention with her unapologetic insistence that women were the equals of men. This was a radical idea at the time. "I have plowed and planted . . . I could work as much and eat as much as a man, (when I could get it) and bear de lash as well," declared Sojourner. She spoke from experience shared by none of her listeners. By emphasizing her past as a slave, Sojourner linked the women's rights cause to the other focus of her life, the abolitionist movement. Up until the Civil War, Sojourner traveled and spoke out as an abolitionist and women's rights activist.

Today, we remember Sojourner Truth primarily for her "Ain't I a woman?" speech. But she was remarkable for many of her achievements. In spite of being an African American woman, Sojourner came to be respected as a celebrity in an age when society considered women and African Americans inferior to white men. When she gained her freedom, instead of settling down to enjoy it, Sojourner became a traveling preacher and an activist. She never let hostile audiences nor personal hardships deter her. After the Civil War, she helped freedmen in Washington, D.C. Even in her eighties, Sojourner traveled to Kansas to support refugee freedmen.

History has not preserved well Sojourner Truth's landmark speech. There is no reliable record of the exact words that she spoke in Akron. Being unable to read or write, Sojourner did not have a prepared speech, and by all accounts, she spoke from the heart. In addition, the Akron convention is largely ignored in the story of the women's rights movement, except for having been the platform for Sojourner's address. However, the lack of documentation does not mute the meaning and importance of what she said that day. Sojourner Truth's life and words stand as an inspiration to everyone who fights for justice and equal rights today.

+≈ CHAPTER 1 ≈+

A NATION OF INEQUALITY

Sojourner Truth was born in rural New York, sometime
around 1797. Her parents, like most black Americans
at the time, were both slaves. At the time of
Sojourner's birth, less than a decade after the United States
ratified the Constitution, slavery had already become a
contentious issue in the young country. Many people con-
demned the institution and called for all slaves to be freed.
Slaveholders vigorously defended slavery, especially in the
southern United States.

Slavery took root in the American colonies during the
first half of the seventeenth century. It developed differently
in the Northern and Southern colonies. Agriculture sus-
tained the Southern economy, and agriculture depended on
slave labor. Slaves worked on huge plantations, tending com-
mercial crops such as cotton, tobacco, rice, and sugarcane.
Small landowners often owned only a handful of slaves; the
owners of large plantations could own hundreds.

The Northern economy was far less dependent on slave
labor. Slaves in the North worked on small farms, in private
homes, or in small businesses or industries. Although slaves

In general, there were two types of slaves: household slaves and field slaves. While both types of slaves were found all across the United States during the eighteenth and nineteenth centuries, the vast majority of the slaves in the South were field slaves while many of the slaves in the North were household slaves. A household slave is depicted holding a white child in the top photograph, while a family of field slaves is shown in the bottom photograph.

made up a large proportion of the population in some areas, Northern slaves were more likely to be isolated from other blacks. Many Northern slaveholders owned only one or two slaves.

During the American Revolution (1775–1783), patriotic Americans championed the cause of liberty. Many people believed that the ideals in the Declaration of Independence conflicted with the realities of slavery. Some of the Founding Fathers, including George Washington, freed their slaves or granted them freedom in their wills. After the revolution, Northern states began taking measures to restrict or eliminate slavery. Vermont became the first state to ban slavery in 1777.

The framers of the U.S. Constitution compromised on the issue of slavery. They did so because Southern slaveholders threatened to withdraw from the Union if the institution was threatened. The Constitution stated that a slave counted as "three-fifths" of a person in population statistics. It authorized the enactment of fugitive slave laws so that owners could reclaim escaped slaves. A clause allowed the foreign slave trade to continue for twenty years after the drafting of the Constitution. Congress outlawed the foreign slave trade in 1808.

By the time Sojourner was born, every Northern state except New York and New Jersey had eliminated slavery. In 1799, the New York legislature decreed that all slaves born after July 4, 1799, would eventually be freed—women would gain their freedom at age twenty-five and men at twenty-eight. An 1817 law established that slaves born before 1799 would be freed on July 4, 1827.

Even as the North gradually abolished slavery, the practice became more deeply entrenched in the South. Slave owners argued that slavery was necessary for the health of the economy. They increasingly claimed that it benefited both masters and slaves. By the mid-nineteenth century, Southern slaveholders generally rejected the idea in the Declaration of Independence that "all men are created equal." Southern

ANTISLAVERY VIOLENCE

The abolitionist movement grew out of religious and nonviolent roots. However, many Southern slaveholders feared that freed or escaped slaves might trigger an uprising large enough to destroy the plantation system. During the early nineteenth century, several unsuccessful slave revolts reinforced their fear. Gabriel's Rebellion was led by a slave named Gabriel Prosser in 1800. Prosser recruited over a thousand armed slaves and planned to capture Richmond, Virginia. The rebellion ended when a sudden downpour washed out a bridge that the slaves had planned to use. In 1822, a free African American preacher named Denmark Vesey organized a massive revolt in South Carolina. It was foiled by an informer. In 1831 in Virginia, a slave and preacher named Nat Turner began one of the most famous uprisings. He and a handful of followers terrorized white plantation owners for more than two months before he was finally captured.

leaders such as John C. Calhoun claimed that slaves, being of African descent, were naturally inferior to whites. According to Calhoun, the slave system created a stable foundation for society. He also argued that slaves would be worse off if they were freed.

The Abolitionist Movement

A major point of contention between the North and the South was the prospect of allowing slavery in the western territories. Northerners,

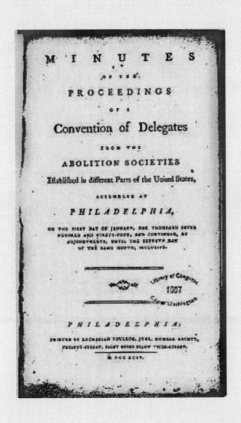

This is the title page of the minutes of an abolitionist convention held in Philadelphia on January 1, 1794. The convention was attended by representatives from abolition societies in Connecticut, Delaware, Maryland, New Jersey, New York, and Pennsylvania. The delegates voted to petition Congress to ban the slave trade and to lobby various state legislatures to abolish slavery altogether.

especially those in the Free-Soil movement, wanted to reserve the territories for independent settlers in search of new opportunities. Southerners believed that the slave system should be allowed to expand. They felt that if slavery were banned in the West, antislavery advocates might try to completely abolish slavery. A series of compromises kept the United States from falling apart over the issue. Yet neither side felt that the matter had been satisfactorily resolved.

The abolitionist movement in the North began with religious revivals and antislavery sentiments within religious groups such as the Quakers. In 1831, an abolitionist named William Lloyd Garrison founded the abolitionist newspaper *The Liberator*. He helped establish the American Anti-Slavery Society in 1833. By the 1840s, abolitionists had organized the Underground Railroad, an antislavery network that helped escaped slaves on their journey toward freedom. Although a relatively small percentage of Americans took an active part in the abolitionist movement, abolitionists made their cause a national issue.

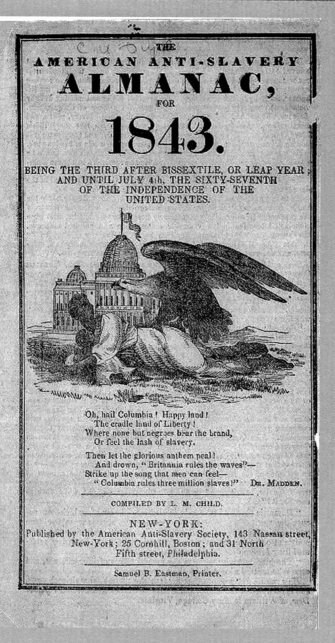

THE
AMERICAN ANTI-SLAVERY
ALMANAC,
FOR
1843.

BEING THE THIRD AFTER BISSEXTILE, OR LEAP YEAR;
AND UNTIL JULY 4th, THE SIXTY-SEVENTH
OF THE INDEPENDENCE OF THE
UNITED STATES.

Oh, hail Columbia! Happy land!
  The cradle land of Liberty!
Where none but negroes bear the brand,
  Or feel the lash of slavery.

Then let the glorious anthem peal!
  And drown, "Britannia rules the waves"—
Strike up the song that men can feel—
  "Columbia rules three million slaves!"   DR. MADDEN.

COMPILED BY L. M. CHILD.

NEW-YORK:
Published by the American Anti-Slavery Society, 143 Nassau street,
New-York; 25 Cornhill, Boston; and 31 North
Fifth street, Philadelphia.

Samuel B. Eastman, Printer.

This abolitionist almanac was published by the American Anti-Slavery Society in 1843. It includes poems, drawings, essays, and other abolitionist propaganda that brought attention to the plight of slaves. It was commissioned by William Lloyd Garrison and compiled by Lydia Maria Child, who edited the New York–based *National Anti-Slavery Standard* newspaper between 1841 and 1849.

The South reacted defensively to abolitionist efforts. Southern slave owners refused to acknowledge the abolitionists' appeals and often banned antislavery publications. Some Southerners believed that the movement was a Northern plot for social, political, and economic dominance. They claimed that abolishing slavery would destroy the agricultural way of life in the South. Even before the abolitionist movement gained a foothold in the North, political extremists in the South threatened to secede from the Union if they felt that their lifestyle and livelihoods were in peril.

Tensions between the North and South increased after the 1850 Fugitive Slave Act was passed. The measure allowed Southern slaveholders to track down and seize runaway slaves, even when the slaves had escaped to the North. The rift between the two sides widened throughout the 1850s, leading to the secession of eleven Southern states from the Union and eventually the Civil War (1861–1865).

The Women's Rights Movement

Many white women joined the abolitionist movement as it spread during the 1830s. They were frustrated that they were not fully allowed to participate. In many meetings, only men were allowed to speak. Women were not always permitted to sign resolutions. In 1840, a number of Americans traveled to London for the World Anti-Slavery Convention. Several of the delegates were women, including the famous speaker Lucretia Mott. When they arrived, many British and American men objected to the women speaking or even attending. The women were told to sit behind a curtain in a gallery.

Mott and some other delegates, both male and female, were outraged. Mott met a young woman named Elizabeth Cady Stanton at the convention. They decided to organize a conference that would focus on

At top, an engraving depicting Lucretia Mott and another early suffragette being protected from an angry male mob, which had broken up a women's rights meeting in the 1840s. At bottom, a photograph of Susan B. Anthony and Elizabeth Cady Stanton, cofounders of the National Woman Suffrage Association, around 1881.

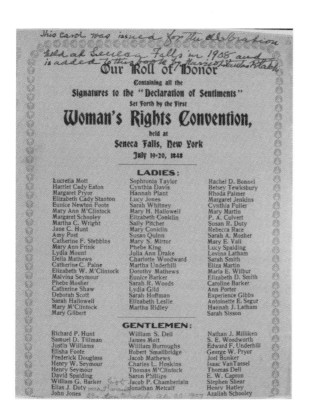

This page from the Declaration of Sentiments is entitled "Our Roll of Honor." It lists the names of the Seneca Falls convention delegates who signed the document. The Declaration of Sentiments was signed by sixty-eight women and thirty-two men.

women's rights. They held the first women's rights convention at Seneca Falls, New York, in 1848. About 300 people, including forty men, arrived on the first day. They discussed controversial issues such as property and divorce laws, access to jobs and education, and suffrage, the right to vote. The organizers had drafted a Declaration of Sentiments based on the Declaration of Independence. The Declaration of Sentiments included a list of twelve resolutions on women's issues, including one that demanded the right to vote. It was signed by approximately 100 people.

Newspapers treated the convention as a joke. Even many abolitionists refused to take women's rights seriously. However, some, like William Lloyd Garrison, supported the cause. But while most men laughed, the women's rights movement spread. Women across the country established women's rights groups. More conventions and meetings followed the historic Seneca Falls convention.

CHAPTER 2

A JOURNEY OUT OF SLAVERY

I t was sometime during the late 1790s that a slave named Isabella was born in the village of Hurley, New York, near the Hudson River. Her master, Colonel Johannes Hardenbergh, did not record the exact date. Later in her life, Isabella would change her name to Sojourner Truth.

Isabella's parents were named Elizabeth and James. They are sometimes referred to as Mau-Mau Bett and Baumfree, meaning "tree" in Dutch. Isabella was probably Elizabeth's tenth or twelfth child, but at the time of her birth, every other sibling except for one older brother had been sold to other masters. Isabella's parents lived in sorrow over their lost children and apprehension that they would lose their remaining son and daughter.

Colonel Hardenbergh belonged to a wealthy Dutch family of slaveholders that had lived on the land for nearly a century. He owned six or seven slaves, more than the typical New York farmer. Because Isabella grew up in a Dutch-speaking community, she learned Dutch as her first language. When she was very young, Colonel Hardenbergh died and his son, Charles, inherited his farm and slaves.

In 1807 or 1808, Charles Hardenbergh died, and much of his property, including Isabella and her brother, was auctioned off. The Hardenbergh family decided to free James because he was too old to work and was no longer an economic asset. They also freed Elizabeth so that she could care for him. James and Elizabeth lived in wretched poverty, and both died within a few years.

A storekeeper named John Nealy paid $100 for Isabella and a flock of sheep. His family spoke only English, and they cruelly whipped Isabella when she did not understand orders. She carried the scars for the rest of her life. Somehow, her father helped arrange for Martin Scriver, a fisherman and innkeeper, to buy her.

Isabella spent her days with the Scrivers gardening, carrying fish, and running errands. They were kinder masters than the Nealys were, and Isabella picked up English more quickly. In 1810, the Scrivers sold her to a farmer named John Dumont.

The four other slaves of the household considered Dumont a decent master. Isabella was very anxious to please him, and her attitude toward him sometimes verged on worship. He praised Isabella's hard work. However, as was customary at the time, he did sometimes beat her despite her efforts. The other slaves taunted Isabella for her attachment to Dumont. They told her that she should not work so eagerly for an owner who kept her enslaved.

When Isabella was sixteen or seventeen, she fell in love with a slave named Robert, who worked on a neighboring farm. His master forbade him to visit Isabella. One day, when he sneaked away to see her, his owner followed and nearly beat him to death. Dumont intervened, unwilling to have blood spilled on his land. Robert's master led him away and eventually married him to one of his own slaves. Isabella never saw Robert again. Soon afterward, Dumont married her to a fellow slave named Thomas. Isabella had five children between 1815 and 1826.

Entitled *Isabella Among the Flock*, this oil painting by Ed Wong-Longda imagines Sojourner Truth on the auction block with a flock of sheep. Sojourner wrote in her autobiography that the Hardenbergh family sought to increase the bids for her by adding sheep to the proposed transaction.

Under New York law, Isabella would be freed on July 4, 1827. Dumont told her that if she worked extra hard, he would free her a year early. Isabella kept her part of the bargain, even though she had severely injured her hand. When July 4, 1826, arrived, Dumont claimed that her injury had prevented her from putting in enough work and he refused to free her.

Freedom and Hard Times

Isabella stayed with the Dumonts until late 1826. Late one night, she left with her baby Sophia, believing that God was directing her. She found her way to the Van Wagenens, a nearby antislavery family. When Dumont tracked her down, she told him that she would rather go to jail than return to him. The Van Wagenens paid $25 for the freedom of Isabella and her baby. She worked for the Van Wagenens as a free woman for the next year.

In 1827, Isabella learned that her six-year-old son, Peter, had been sold and taken to Alabama. It was illegal to sell New York slaves to Southern owners. New York was slowly abolishing slavery, but in Alabama, Peter would likely be enslaved for life. Isabella took a course of action that was almost unheard of for a black woman in those days. She filed a complaint in court. A jury decided in her favor, and in 1828, Peter was returned to her. His owner had whipped and beaten him until he was covered with scars from head to toe.

A year later, Isabella and Peter left for New York City. Isabella left her other children behind with the Dumonts. In New York City, she worked as a housekeeper in private homes. Isabella also became actively involved in the Methodist Church. She had become a Methodist soon after gaining her freedom. Isabella was a deeply religious person. She threw her whole soul into spreading her faith by preaching, praying, and singing.

MATTHEWS, *alias* MATTHIAS,

CHARGED WITH HAVING

Swindled Mr. B. H. Folger,

OF THE CITY OF NEW-YORK,

OUT OF CONSIDERABLE PROPERTY:

WITH THE

Speeches of Counsel, and Opinion of the Court on the motion of the District Attorney, that a Nolle Prosequi be entered in the Case.

ALSO,

A Sketch of the Impostor's Character,

And a detailed History of his Career as a "Prophet," together with many other Particulars, which have not hitherto been published.

BY W. E. DRAKE, CONGRESSIONAL AND LAW REPORTER.

NEW-YORK: PRINTED AND PUBLISHED BY W. MITCHELL, 265 BOWERY, And may be had of him, and all the Booksellers.

Benjamin Folger, one of the founding members of Matthias's Kingdom, published this book about the abuses carried out by its leader, Robert Matthews, against members of the religious sect. In it, Folger accused Matthews of being a swindler and called Sojourner Truth an evil witch. Sojourner won a $125 judgment against Folger for slander and libel.

Isabella gained a reputation as a stirring preacher. She often spoke at religious meetings. Soon after moving to New York City, she met a religious fanatic named Elijah Pierson while working at a women's shelter. Pierson drew Isabella into a cult led by Robert Matthews. He called his small community Matthias's Kingdom. Isabella gave the group all of her money and did much of the cooking and housework. Matthews treated his followers like servants, though he himself dressed finely and drank from a silver goblet.

In 1834, Pierson died suddenly, and Matthews was accused of poisoning him. Newspapers revealed Matthews as an impostor and publicized some of the cult's bizarre rituals. Though Isabella had not been involved, two members of Matthias's Kingdom made false accusations against her. She sued them for slander and cleared her name in court.

While Isabella was involved in Matthias's Kingdom, her son Peter had been getting into trouble. He could not keep a job and was often caught stealing. His mother thought that an education might give him more opportunities, but he skipped school to go dancing. In 1839, Peter signed on as a seaman on a whaling ship. Isabella never saw her son again. They exchanged a few letters up until 1841, but Isabella never learned what happened to Peter after that.

In 1843, Isabella decided to leave New York City. She thought it was a wicked city. Also, she claimed to have been called by God to spread her faith. Isabella quit her job as a domestic. She told her employer that her name was no longer Isabella but Sojourner Truth. Sojourner planned to travel all over the country, preaching to the people she encountered.

An Abolitionist and Feminist

Sojourner spent the next few months traveling and speaking at religious meetings. During this time, a religious fervor called the Second Great Awakening was sweeping the country. People attended meetings to pray, listen to speakers, and reaffirm their faith. Sojourner's preaching and stories often led listeners to laugh and cry. They appreciated her plain speaking and wit. Sojourner also sang hymns she had written herself.

When winter came, Sojourner settled down in Northampton, Massachusetts. She joined the Northampton Association, a cooperative community that believed in equality for all people. Many of the members were involved in the abolitionist movement. George Benson, a brother-in-law of the abolitionist William Lloyd Garrison, was one of the leaders. Garrison himself often visited Northampton, as did ex-slave and abolitionist Frederick Douglass.

Douglass wrote his autobiography, *Narrative of the Life of Frederick Douglass, An American Slave*, in 1845. It sold very well, and his success

NARRATIVE
OF
SOJOURNER TRUTH;

A Bondswoman of Olden Time,

EMANCIPATED BY THE NEW YORK LEGISLATURE IN THE EARLY
PART OF THE PRESENT CENTURY;

WITH A HISTORY OF HER

Labors and Correspondence,

DRAWN FROM HER

"BOOK OF LIFE."

BOSTON:
PUBLISHED FOR THE AUTHOR.
1875.

Narrative of Sojourner Truth chronicles Sojourner's experiences as a Northern slave and tells of the spiritual transformation that inspired her to travel across the United States to speak out against slavery and other social inequalities. It is one of the earliest accounts of the life of a female slave. The cover and title page from an 1875 revision are pictured here. The book was first published in 1850.

This photograph shows Frederick Douglass (seated beside the woman with the white bonnet) at the Great Cazenovia Fugitive Slave Law Convention in Cazenovia, New York, in 1850. More than 2,000 people, including about fifty runaway slaves, attended the abolitionist event. Douglass escaped from slavery in 1838.

inspired Sojourner to publish her own autobiography. Because she could not read or write, she dictated her story to a friend named Olive Gilbert. Garrison helped publish *Narrative of Sojourner Truth* in 1850. Sojourner hoped that she could sell copies of her book when she spoke at meetings. The Northampton Association had closed in 1846, and she had bought a house near Northampton. She needed money to pay the mortgage.

In October 1850, Sojourner attended a women's rights conference in Worcester, Massachusetts. Many of her old friends from Northampton also attended. Here, Sojourner made her first documented speech as an activist, arguing for women's rights. In November, she made her first known antislavery speech. Wherever Sojourner spoke, she offered copies of her book for sale. It is quite possible that Sojourner had spoken out on the issues of abolition and women's rights earlier, but there is no documentary proof.

After the Worcester convention, Garrison invited Sojourner to join him and a British abolitionist, George Thompson, on a speaking tour. When Sojourner arrived in Springfield, Massachusetts, to begin the tour, she found that Garrison had fallen ill. He had stayed at home in Boston to recover. Sojourner could not afford to go on tour without Garrison's financial help, and she explained the situation to Thompson. He offered to pay her way and treated her as an equal.

In 1851, Sojourner met Isaac and Amy Post, longtime abolitionists and activists for women's rights. It was the start of a lifelong friendship. Sojourner stayed with the Posts for much of the winter before heading to Ohio. She planned to attend antislavery meetings and a women's rights conference in Akron.

                                      ✦═ **CHAPTER 3** ═✦

"AIN'T I A WOMAN?"

I n 1851, Ohio was deeply divided over the issue of slavery. Ohio was a free state bordering Southern slave states. The Underground Railroad was particularly active in Ohio. Many runaway slaves headed north to the state border and freedom. At the same time, new Ohio laws prohibited escaped slaves from entering or settling in the state. The slavery debate intensified across the country with the 1850 passage of the Fugitive Slave Act. Abolitionists denounced the law. Many traveled through Ohio speaking out against the practice of slavery and the Fugitive Slave Act.

Women as well as men were drawn to the antislavery movement. As they fought for the abolitionist cause, some of the activists also began calling for women's rights. They believed in equality for all people, whether they were white or black, male or female.

In the spring of 1851, Sojourner spent time in Salem, Ohio, an antislavery town. She stayed with Emily and Marius Robinson, who were abolitionists and friends of William Lloyd Garrison. They ran the *Anti-Slavery Bugle*, the only abolitionist paper in the area. The *Bugle* also reported on

I Sell the Shadow to Support the Substance.
SOJOURNER TRUTH.

Sojourner Truth sold calling cards such as the one pictured here to help finance her reformist activities. Most of them bore the slogan "I sell the shadow to support the substance."

women's rights issues. In March 1851, it urged all reformers to attend a women's rights convention in Akron.

Frances D. Gage organized the Akron conference. It took place in late May. Sojourner was the only black person in attendance. A religious group, the Universalists, allowed the conference to meet in its church. Gage was a writer of fiction and poetry, and an ardent supporter of both the abolitionist and women's rights movements. She wrote an account of Sojourner's Akron address that made the "Ain't I a woman?" speech a legend. Some historians, however, believe that Gage may have added her own words to the text and changed details of the event to make the story more dramatic.

Gage's Telling of "Ain't I a Woman?"

Sojourner Truth was illiterate. Although friends and listeners recorded many of her speeches, Sojourner never wrote down her own words. By all reports, she was a moving and charismatic speaker. Today, we will never be able to grasp any more than a shadow of what Sojourner's audience must have experienced.

Frances Gage wrote her account of Sojourner's "Ain't I a woman?" speech in 1863, twelve years after the Akron convention. She published it in the *National Anti-Slavery Standard*, a New York abolitionist newspaper. Sojourner later included Gage's article in an updated version of *Narrative of Sojourner Truth*.

Gage opens her account with a description of the general hostility of many Americans to the women's rights movement. She uses formal, flowery prose typical of the nineteenth century. Describing Sojourner's arrival at the church, Gage writes of "seeing a tall, gaunt black woman in a gray dress and white turban, surmounted by an uncouth sun-bonnet, march deliberately into the church, [and] walk with the air of a queen up the aisle." Gage claims that many people were disturbed by a black woman taking part in the conference. She reports that they entreated, "Don't let her speak, Mrs. G. It will ruin us. Every newspaper in the land will have our cause mixed up with abolition." Gage replied merely, "We will see when the time comes."

Sojourner made her speech on the second day of the conference. According to Gage's account, most of the morning had been dominated by men, especially clergymen, arguing the inferiority of women. The audience was unfriendly to the women's rights movement, and the women were afraid to defend their cause. Finally, unasked, Sojourner stood up and moved to the front of the room. Despite the disapproval of the audience, Gage stood up and announced her: "Sojourner Truth." According to Gage's account, "Every eye was fixed on this almost Amazon form, which stood nearly six feet high, head erect, and eye piercing the upper air like one in a dream . . . She spoke in deep tones, which, though not loud, reached every ear in the house."

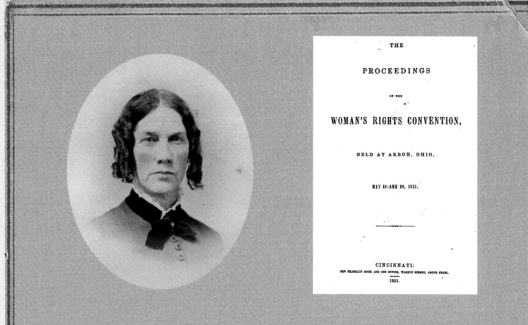

Frances Gage was born in Washington County, Ohio, in 1808. The mother of eight children, she did not become an activist until the early 1840s, when she began writing for a newspaper. As president of the Akron convention, she delivered the opening address, which is documented in the published minutes of the convention *(right)*. In it, she declared that if women united to speak for themselves, "they would ameliorate mankind" and "purify, elevate and ennoble humanity."

Sojourner opened her speech by pointing out the "racket" over inequality being raised by both antislavery and women's rights advocates. As a black woman, Sojourner uniquely represented both causes. "Well, chillen," Sojourner began, "Whar dar's so much racket dar must be som'ting out o' kilter. I tink dat, 'twixt the niggers of de south and de women at de norf, all a-talking 'bout rights, de white men will be in a fix pretty soon." She then gestured to a man in the audience. "Dat man over dar say dat woman needs to be helped into carriages, and lifted over ditches, and to have de best place eberywhar. Nobody eber

SOJOURNER SPEAKS

"It is impossible to transfer it to paper, or convey any adequate idea of the effect it produced upon the audience," wrote Sojourner's friend Marius Robinson after her "Ain't I a woman?" speech. He referred in part to her compelling charisma, but he also had a practical difficulty in transcribing Sojourner's words: her accent.

Many people recorded her speeches in a Southern dialect, thinking that readers would expect a former slave to speak with a Southern accent. But Sojourner grew up in the North and spoke Dutch as her first language. She probably retained traces of Dutch mannerisms in her speech for her whole life. John Dumont's daughter Gertrude claimed that Sojourner's accent resembled that of the typical uneducated farmer in New York State. According to Frederick Douglass, Sojourner "cared very little for elegance of speech," but she easily captivated an audience.

helps me into carriages, or ober mud-puddles, or gives me any best place . . . And ar'n't I a woman?" In Gage's account, Sojourner dramatically repeats "Ar'n't I a woman?" four times through her speech. Modern reprints often change it to "Ain't I a woman?"

Sojourner went on to refute the widely held belief that women were weaker than men. "I have plowed and planted and gathered into barns, and no man could head me . . . I could work as much and eat as much as a man—when I could get it—and bear de lash as well." For the listeners in Akron, Sojourner stood as living proof that women were no less capable than men. Her words also alluded to the evils of slavery and the hardships she had endured.

Sojourner used a metaphor to attack the idea that women were intellectually inferior to men. "If my cup won't hold but a pint and yourn holds a quart, wouldn't ye be mean not to let me have my little half-measure full?" Sojourner meant that despite physical differences, such as size, women were not less intelligent than men. Therefore, men should not deny women equal rights on the claim that they were not smart enough to make responsible decisions.

According to Gage, Sojourner next singled out a minister in the audience. "Den dat little man in black dar, he say woman can't have as much right as man 'cause Christ wa'n't a woman. Whar did your Christ come from? From God and a woman." She argued that if Eve had truly brought sin to the world, then women should be given the chance to "turn it back and git it right side up again." The audience applauded after each of Sojourner's points. Summing up the experience, Gage says, "I have never in my life seen anything like the magical influence that subdued the mobbish spirit of the day, and turned the jibes and sneers of an excited crowd into notes of respect and admiration."

Other Accounts

There is no doubt that Frances D. Gage's account captured the spirit and message of Sojourner's speech. In her version, Sojourner calls for equal rights and refers to experiences of her own life. She quotes the Bible, as she did in many other speeches. Although she never learned to read, Sojourner memorized long passages from the Bible.

Many historians studying Sojourner Truth doubt parts of Gage's account. Most agree on one main point: Gage exaggerated the hostile

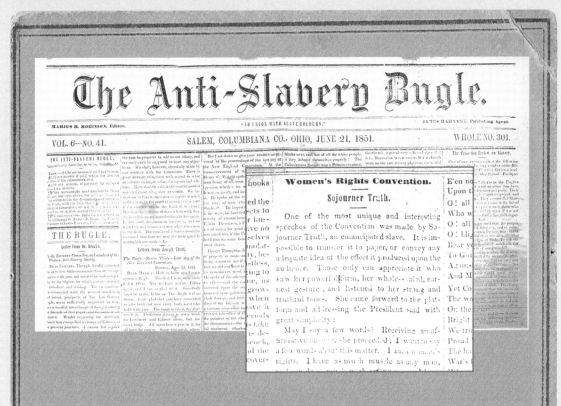

This June 21, 1851, edition of the Salem, Ohio, *Anti-Slavery Bugle* carried a favorable account of the Akron convention. Published by well-known abolitionists Benjamin and Jane Elizabeth Jones, the *Bugle* was one of the most influential antislavery newspapers of its time.

atmosphere of the Akron women's rights conference. Gage describes a stirring turnaround, but in reality, it is unlikely that Sojourner truly addressed an unfriendly audience.

The general consensus among historians is that men and women who attended the Akron convention were supportive of the women's rights movement and the abolitionist cause. Some were Sojourner's close personal friends. The town of Akron welcomed the convention and the local community offered the use of its church for the event. Afterward, twenty-seven newspapers featured accounts of the events, four of them

31

describing Sojourner's speech. No published report mentions any discord. Some attendees publicly stated that they were delighted with the harmony of the conference and their reception at Akron.

Sojourner faced hostile audiences many times in her life. However, it is likely that she was surrounded by friendly faces at Akron. Women's rights conferences during the nineteenth century generally welcomed black speakers. Frederick Douglass spoke at the historic 1848 Seneca Falls convention in New York, and Sojourner attended many other women's rights conferences over the next couple of decades.

It is doubtful that antifeminist men dominated the stage on the day Sojourner spoke, as Gage claimed. Her friend and host Marius Robinson acted as recording secretary for the conference. He wrote in the *Bugle* that "the business of the convention was principally conducted by women," a statement reiterated in other newspapers. Participants probably debated how far equal rights should extend for women, however, and Sojourner may have addressed some of their points in her speech.

In Gage's account, Sojourner emerged as the star of the conference. Other newspaper articles reported that a number of women spoke powerfully and together made the convention a success. Robinson also wrote a detailed account of Sojourner's speech. Carleton Mabee, author of a biography of Sojourner Truth, believes that Robinson's report is probably the most authentic record of the speech. Robinson does not mention any hostility. In his account, Sojourner politely asks, "May I speak a few words?" before beginning. Robinson transcribed Sojourner's words in proper English rather than the dialect Gage used. Much of his content agrees with Gage's version.

A few historians have questioned the accuracy of Gage's text. She admits, "I have given but a faint sketch of her speech," without mentioning her source. Her version contains one glaring inaccuracy: "I

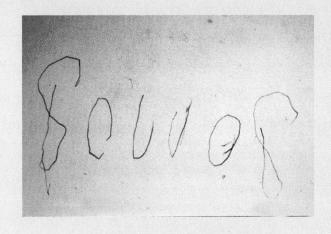

On April 23, 1880, Sojourner Truth signed her name in the autograph book of a Michigan schoolgirl named Hattie Johnson. The signature is the only known example of writing by Sojourner, who never learned to read or write.

have borne thirteen chillen, and seen 'em mos' all sold off into slavery." (Sojourner had only five children.) Some scholars even believe that Gage, not Sojourner, coined the slogan "Ain't I a woman?" Gage reported that Sojourner repeated the phrase four times, yet no other account mentions the words "Ain't I a woman?"

Sojourner is not known to have used the phrase in any other speech, nor did she have a habit of repeating key phrases when she spoke. Gage, however, was a poet and often repeated phrases for emphasis and rhythmic flow. If Sojourner did use the phrase "Ain't I a woman?" it is likely that Gage, not Sojourner herself, turned it into a recurring refrain throughout the speech.

Newspapers gave a glowing report of the conference and applauded Sojourner's speech. Sojourner was also pleased, though she never mentioned the public reaction to her speech. She sent a letter to her friend Amy Post, telling her that she had met many kind friends. "I sold a good many books at the convention and have thus far been greatly prospered." She was slowly paying off her debts, and she soon continued on her speaking tour.

+≡= CHAPTER 4 =≡+

WAR AND EMANCIPATION

The debate over slavery brought the country to a crisis during the 1850s. Abolitionists and extremist Southern leaders dominated the political scene and the differences between them continued to grow. The Senate passed the Kansas-Nebraska Act in 1854. The act specified that the citizens of a territory should choose whether or not to allow slavery. Senator Stephen Douglas of Illinois had intended the act to heal relations between slaveholders and abolitionists, but the gap only widened.

Feelings intensified when the Supreme Court ruled on the case of *Dred Scott v. John F. A. Sandford*. The Dred Scott decision stated that slaveholders had the right to take their slaves into free states and keep them enslaved. Slaveholders considered the case a major victory, but it spurred the abolitionist movement. In 1859, a white abolitionist named John Brown and several followers seized a federal arsenal at Harpers Ferry in present-day West Virginia. Though Brown's effort to start a slave rebellion failed, he alarmed local governments throughout the South.

Abraham Lincoln was opposed to the spread of slavery beyond the South. However, he did not advocate an immediate end to slavery until 1863, during the Civil War. This engraving by Alexander Hay Ritchie depicts President Abraham Lincoln presenting the Emancipation Proclamation to members of his cabinet.

The presidential election of 1860 forced a final showdown between the two sides. The abolitionist-supported Republican candidate, Abraham Lincoln, defeated three other men to become the sixteenth president of the United States. Within three months of his March 4, 1861, inauguration, eleven states had seceded from the Union and the Civil War was underway.

Sojourner did not actively participate in politics. After delivering her speech in Akron, she continued her lecture tours. In 1853,

Sojourner traveled to Massachusetts and visited Harriet Beecher Stowe, the famous author of the antislavery novel *Uncle Tom's Cabin*. Sojourner also attended meetings of a new religion called Spiritualism. Many of Sojourner's friends were Spiritualists, and Sojourner may have cared as much about seeing her old friends as the religion itself.

In 1857, Sojourner sold her house in Northampton and bought one in the Spiritualist community of Harmonia, Michigan. She later moved to the nearby town of Battle Creek, where her daughters and grandchildren gathered around her. Though Sojourner spent much time away traveling, Battle Creek was her home for the rest of her life.

Throughout her years as an activist, Sojourner supported the nonviolent abolition of slavery. In 1861, shortly after the war broke out, a group of pro-Confederacy Democrats tried to arrest her during a speaking tour in Indiana. A new Indiana law forbade blacks from entering the state. A pro-Union military group called the Home Guard protected her, but Sojourner insisted on speaking at a courthouse rally as scheduled. Friends dressed her in red, white, and blue, and advised that she carry a sword or pistol. Sojourner answered, as written in her autobiography, "I carry no weapon; the Lord will [preserve] me without weapons."

Some abolitionists began to believe during the 1850s that a peaceful solution could never succeed. Although Sojourner never lost her faith in nonviolence, she proudly supported the Union during the Civil War. One of her grandsons served in the military. Sojourner went door to door collecting food and clothing for local troops. According to legend, one man refused to give her any donations, and she asked his name. "I am the only son of my mother," he replied. "I am glad there are no more," she shot back, with her characteristic sharp wit.

At left, William Wetmore Story's sculpture *Libyan Sibyl*; at right, a page from the April 1863 *Atlantic Monthly* with Harriet Beecher Stowe's article "Sojourner Truth, the Libyan Sibyl." Both tributes to the abolitionist and women's rights activist helped advance the almost mythical view of Sojourner Truth in American history.

The "Libyan Sibyl" and Fame

Sojourner's fame spread as she traveled around the country. People heard her speak, they bought *Narrative of Sojourner Truth*, and they read about her in abolitionist newspapers. Through an odd set of circumstances, she also became widely known as the "Libyan Sibyl."

In the late 1850s, Harriet Beecher Stowe spent her winters in Rome, Italy. There, she met a sculptor named William Wetmore Story. Stowe recounted some of Sojourner's stories to the sculptor. Stowe claimed that her descriptions of Sojourner inspired Story to sculpt a marble statue of an African woman. He called the piece the *Libyan Sibyl* after a mythological figure.

Stowe published an article titled "Sojourner Truth, the Libyan Sibyl" in 1863. Although she admired Sojourner, Stowe portrays her as naive and a passive stereotype instead of giving an honest description of her vibrant personality. The article describes Sojourner's 1853 visit to Andover and tells of her early life. Stowe also relates the story of a confrontation with Frederick Douglass at a meeting in Boston. He had become frustrated with the abolitionist movement and was beginning to think that violence could be the only solution. Sojourner leaped up and cried, "Frederick, is God dead?" Her words shocked the room into silence. The phrase became famous as an affirmation of God's justice.

Stowe's article is filled with inaccuracies, though. Even the famous incident with Douglass did not occur exactly as she describes it. Sojourner later grumbled that she was not from Africa, nor did she ever call anyone "honey," as Stowe claimed. Worst of all, Stowe seemed to think that Sojourner Truth was dead.

Frances D. Gage published her version of "Ain't I a woman?" less than a month after "Sojourner Truth, the Libyan Sibyl" appeared. Gage may have wanted to correct Stowe's portrait of Sojourner as a preacher rather than activist. At one point in her account, however, Gage describes Sojourner as "quiet and reticent as the 'Libyan statue.'" Stowe's article, however, made Sojourner a romanticized celebrity, and many Americans now knew her—and sympathized with her—as the Libyan Sibyl.

Washington, D.C.

On January 1, 1863, President Lincoln freed all slaves in the Confederacy with his Emancipation Proclamation. In early 1864, Sojourner's friends raised money for her to travel to Washington,

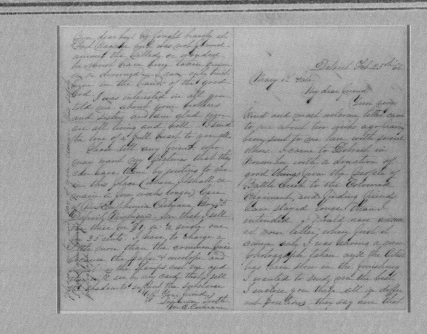

In this letter dated February 25, 1864, Sojourner Truth explains to her friend Mary Gale that she has gone to Detroit to encourage African American Union soldiers. Celebrating the emancipation of slaves, she says, "This is a great and glorious day! It is good to live in it & behold the shackles fall from the manacled limbs. Oh if I were ten years younger I would go down with these soldiers here & be the Mother of the Regiment!"

D.C., and she set out on a tour of the East in the summer. Her beloved fourteen-year-old grandson, Sammy, accompanied her.

When she reached Washington, Sojourner visited the White House and spoke with Abraham Lincoln. She showed the president her "Book of Life," a scrapbook full of newspaper clippings and autographs of people Sojourner admired. President Lincoln signed her book, "For Aunty Sojourner Truth, October 29, 1864. A. Lincoln." Later in her life, Sojourner met Presidents Andrew Johnson and Ulysses S. Grant.

Sojourner did not leave Washington until 1868. She had found a new mission when she met the freedmen, or former slaves.

The Civil War ended in 1865. By the end of that year, the Thirteenth Amendment to the Constitution had been ratified. It outlawed slavery in the United States. Still, freedom offered little security for many freedmen. Most had no money and only meager possessions. Remaining in the South meant enduring so-called black codes, which were laws restricting the rights of blacks to own land and to move about as they pleased. Many began migrating to Northern cities in search of work in the factories, yet even there they faced discrimination.

Freedmen swarmed into Washington even before the war ended. Sojourner joined the refugee relief effort, working with agencies such as the National Freedmen's Relief Association. She lived in a tidy cottage in a camp called Freedmen's Village and helped teach former slaves new skills. Sojourner's great hope was that the freedmen would be able to find jobs and cease relying on government aid.

Sojourner often traveled by streetcar during her time in Washington. Often, the conductors would disregard a black woman signaling the car. On a September day in 1865, a conductor violently tried to push her away, injuring Sojourner's shoulder. She had him arrested for assault and battery. For the third time in her life, Sojourner took a case to court and won.

A Lifelong Activist

The Civil War had changed the nature of activists' causes. Abolitionists had seen their hopes become reality. The Fourteenth Amendment to the Constitution granted black men citizenship, and the Fifteenth Amendment gave them the right to vote. This did not end discrimination against blacks, however, and women of all races were still denied equal rights.

Published in *Frank Leslie's Illustrated Newspaper* on September 22, 1866, this illustration shows a roomful of African American women in a sewing class at the Freedmen's Union Industrial School in Richmond, Virginia. Sojourner worked in institutions such as this one to teach former slaves new skills.

The women's rights movement split into two factions in 1869. The group organized by Elizabeth Cady Stanton and Susan B. Anthony opposed the Fifteenth Amendment if women were not included. The other half of the movement supported the Fifteenth Amendment, believing that black male suffrage was an important step in the fight for equal rights. The groups were also divided on political strategy and a few key issues. Sojourner urged the two groups to mend their differences, but she continued speaking out for women's rights. Finally, she gave her support to the less radical group that supported the Fifteenth Amendment.

THE EXODUSTERS

The last federal troops left the South in 1877, marking the end of Reconstruction. Though the Constitution had guaranteed them freedom and citizenship, freedmen living in the South faced a new era of racial oppression. Whites kept them out of decent-paying jobs, passed laws to keep them from owning land, and used intimidation to keep them from voting. Many freedmen left the South to look for jobs in the Northern cities. Others looked to the Western territories. There, they could own their own farms and establish communities. Leaders such as Benjamin "Pap" Singleton called for an African American exodus to Kansas. The response was huge, as 20,000 freedmen left the South between 1877 and 1879 and settled around the town of Nicodemus. The freedmen, nicknamed Exodusters for taking part in the exodus, established farms under the Homestead Act of 1862, which offered 160 acres of government land to citizens who would cultivate that property for at least five years. Others founded businesses in town. Nicodemus grew quickly and served as a magnet and inspiration to others. By the end of the nineteenth century, communities and towns founded by freedmen dotted the Western prairie.

At top, an African American family is shown posing in front of their home in Nicodemus, Kansas. At bottom, a handbill, issued by Benjamin "Pap" Singleton, founder of the town of Nicodemus, calls on Southern African Americans to take advantage of the homestead program by moving to Kansas.

Sojourner left Washington discouraged by the plight of the freedmen. Jobs were scarce, and many freedmen lacked food and shelter. Sojourner proposed that the government reserve parts of the empty western territories for freedmen settlements. She felt that after generations of slavery, freedmen deserved the chance to cultivate their own land rather than live in poverty in the cities.

Sojourner traveled and spoke out in support of her plan. She even wrote up a petition to present to Congress and collected signatures. In 1871 and 1872, Sojourner and Sammy toured Kansas, Missouri, and the Midwest promoting resettlement. However, Sojourner could not find support in Washington for her expensive proposal. The government was still reeling from the costs of the Civil War and Reconstruction of the South. Racism also played a role, as these areas were primarily settled by whites at the time.

In 1875, bad news brought Sojourner back to Battle Creek. Sammy was gravely ill. He died in February, and Sojourner went into debt to pay for his medical bills and burial. Later in the year, Sojourner's close friend Frances Titus helped publish a new edition of her autobiography, updating Sojourner's history and adding part of the "Book of Life." For many years, Titus helped Sojourner in every way she could and accompanied her on her travels.

To Sojourner's delight, waves of Southern freedmen decided to relocate to the West in an exodus during the late 1870s. Sojourner traveled to Kansas with Titus to help with the relief effort on behalf of the refugees. Her dream for the freedmen had come true.

CHAPTER 5

SOJOURNER TRUTH'S LEGACY

Sojourner and Titus traveled about the Midwest in 1881 and then returned permanently to Battle Creek. Now in her eighties, Sojourner's health was declining. Sojourner Truth died on November 26, 1883. Titus cared for her during her last years of illness and raised money for a monument at her gravesite.

Her friends and fellow activists mourned her and celebrated her memory. "Venerable for age, distinguished for insight into human nature, remarkable for independence and courageous self-assertion, devoted to the welfare of her race, she has been for the last forty years an object of respect and admiration to social reformers everywhere," wrote Frederick Douglass the day after her death. The women's rights activists Elizabeth Cady Stanton and Susan B. Anthony called Sojourner "the most wonderful woman the colored race has ever produced" in their *History of Woman Suffrage*. Frances Titus added "A Memorial Chapter" to *Narrative of Sojourner Truth* in 1884.

Tracing Sojourner's History

During the 1860s, Sojourner began selling small photographs of herself. Many carried the message, "I sell the shadow to support the substance." In the photographs, Sojourner was dressed simply and her head was covered. She sat or stood in a dignified, solemn pose. One shows her with knitting in her lap and a book at her elbow, although she could not read. She was never shown smoking a pipe, one of her vices.

Just as viewers cannot detect Sojourner's dynamic personality from the photographs, historians have a difficult time piecing together her life history from historical documents. Although Sojourner dictated her own story, Olive Gilbert and Frances Titus helped put together *Narrative of Sojourner Truth*. Gilbert inserted her own comments into the text of the book. Titus changed a few details when she added Sojourner's "Book of Life." Newspaper reporters often had their own agendas in mind when writing about Sojourner. Even when they intended to write objectively, their own viewpoints colored their tone. Sojourner's personal correspondence was written by friends, so it is difficult to tell whether her letters preserve her exact words.

Sojourner's life story has always been open to interpretation. During her lifetime, people associated Sojourner most closely with the slogan "Is God dead?" not with the phrase "Ain't I a woman?" "Is God Dead" was even carved onto her tombstone. Like Harriet Beecher Stowe, people may have felt more comfortable thinking of Sojourner as a devout preacher, not as a black female declaring herself the equal of any man. Women's rights activists focused on her work on behalf of women, and abolitionists praised her efforts for the abolitionist cause. Many contemporary accounts of Sojourner's life downplay her strong religious beliefs and family troubles.

The Impact of "Ain't I a Woman?"

The modern image of Sojourner Truth is largely a result of Frances Gage's account. Sojourner stands in our minds as a strong black

This painting is an unknown artist's rendition of Sojourner Truth's meeting with President Abraham Lincoln in 1864. It portrays Lincoln showing Sojourner Truth a Bible that was given to him by an African American community in Baltimore.

woman who bravely faced her opponents with dignity and fire. Her speech has become a similar type of legend as the story of George Washington chopping down the cherry tree and taking responsibility for his actions. Even if the events are more myth than fact, they still influence our view of George Washington and Sojourner Truth.

Without the dramatic background, Sojourner's "Ain't I a woman?" speech still stands firmly as a landmark address. Sojourner straddled both the abolitionist and women's rights movements. By asking "Ain't I a woman?" she demanded acceptance as a black woman at a time

This memorial to Sojourner Truth stands in front of the Ulster County Courthouse in Kingston, New York. It was here that Sojourner won the lawsuit that saved her son from slavery in Alabama. The memorial salutes her as a "woman of indomitable character."

PORTRAYING SOJOURNER TRUTH

In 1893, Frances Titus commissioned an artist named Frank C. Courter to paint a portrait based on Sojourner's visit with Abraham Lincoln. The painting was the first of many images celebrating Sojourner Truth as a symbol of the equal rights cause. Over the years, she has appeared on posters, buttons, a United States postage stamp, and much more.

when society considered blacks and women inferior. By referring to her life as a slave, she reminded the audience that was there solely to support women's rights of the evils of slavery.

Many women's rights activists advocated women's suffrage, legal rights, and expanded job opportunities. Sojourner did not address the practical issues of the women's rights movement at the Akron convention. Instead, she took a much more radical view, declaring that women were the physical and intellectual equals of men. Women of the nineteenth century were bound by strict social customs, and even many activists did not want to appear "unfeminine." Sojourner's conception of equality between men and women was not widely accepted until the twentieth century.

Today, Sojourner Truth stands as a symbol of a strong black woman and of someone who overcame hardship and worked for equal rights. She has been recognized by the National Women's Hall of Fame.

Battle Creek, Michigan, has a Sojourner Truth Memorial Association and a Sojourner Truth Memorial Highway.

But Sojourner's legacy lies in her dedication to activism, not in awards and memorials. Sojourner lived to see slavery abolished, yet African Americans still faced discrimination. Women did not gain the right to vote during Sojourner's lifetime. Sojourner's work served as an inspiration for supporters of equal rights who followed in her footsteps. In 1920, the Nineteenth Amendment to the Constitution granted women the right to vote. Ninety years after Sojourner sued a Washington, D.C., transit company, Rosa Parks's refusal to give up a bus seat inspired fresh support for the cause of equal rights. The civil rights movement of the 1950s and 1960s made great progress in the fight against racial discrimination. Today, activists for equality and social justice still carry on Sojourner's work.

Frances Gage's Version of Sojourner Truth's "Ain't I a Woman?" Speech (Contemporary English Translation)

Well, children, where there is so much racket, there must be something out of kilter. I think that between the Negroes of the South and the women of the North, all talking about rights, the white men will be in a fix pretty soon. But what's all this here talking about?

That man over there says that women need to be helped into carriages, and lifted over ditches, and to have the best place everywhere. Nobody ever helps me into carriages, or over mud puddles, or gives me any best place! And ain't I a woman? Look at me! Look at my arm! I have plowed and planted, and gathered into barns, and no man could outdo me! And ain't I a woman? I could work as much and eat as much as a man—when I could get it—and bear the lash as well! And ain't I a woman? I have borne thirteen children and seen almost all of them sold off to slavery, and when I cried out with a mother's grief, none but Jesus heard me! And ain't I a woman?

Then they talk about this thing in the head; what's this they call it? (someone whispers, "Intellect"). That's it, honey. What's that have to do with women's rights or Negroes' rights? If my cup won't hold but a pint, and yours holds a quart, wouldn't you be mean not to let me have my little half measure full?

Then that little man in black there, he says women can't have as much rights as men, because Christ wasn't a woman! Where did your

Christ come from? Where did your Christ come from? From God and a woman! Man had nothing to do with Him.

If the first woman God ever made was strong enough to turn the world upside down all alone, these women together ought to be able to turn it back, and get it right side up again! And now they are asking to do it, the men better let them.

I'm obliged to you for hearing me, and now old Sojourner ain't got nothing more to say.

Marius Robinson's Version of Sojourner Truth's "Ain't I a Woman?" Speech

I want to say a few words about this matter.

I am for woman's rights. I have as much muscle as any man, and can do as much work as any man. I have plowed and reaped and husked and chopped and mowed, and can any man do more than that? I have heard much about the sexes being equal. I can carry as much as any man, and can eat as much too, if I can get it. I am as strong as any man that is now.

As for intellect, all I can say is, if a woman have a pint, and a man a quart—why can't she have her little pint full? You need not be afraid to give us our rights for fear we will take too much—for we can't take more than our pint'll hold.

The poor men seems to be all in confusion, and don't know what to do. Why children, if you have woman's rights, give it to her and you will feel better. You will have your own rights, and they won't be so much trouble.

I can't read, but I can hear. I have heard the Bible and have learned that Eve caused man to sin. Well, if woman upset the world, do give her a chance to set it right side up again. The Lady has spoken about

Jesus, how he never spurned woman from him, and she was right. When Lazarus died, Mary and Martha came to him with faith and love and besought him to raise their brother. And Jesus wept and Lazarus came forth. And how came Jesus into the world? Through God who created him and the woman who bore him. Man, where was your part?

But the women are coming up blessed be God and a few of the men are coming up with them. But man is in a tight place, the poor slave is on him, woman is coming on him, he is surely between a hawk and a buzzard.

TIMELINE

ca. 1797 Sojourner Truth is born a slave named Isabella.

1810 Isabella is sold to the Dumont family.

1814 Isabella marries a slave named Thomas.

1815–1826 Isabella bears five children.

1826 Isabella leaves the Dumonts.

1827 Isabella sues to recover her son Peter, who had been sold into slavery in Alabama.

1829 Isabella moves to New York City.

1832 Isabella joins Matthias's Kingdom.

1843 Isabella leaves New York and takes the name Sojourner Truth.

1844 Sojourner Truth settles in Northampton, Massachusetts.

1850 Sojourner publishes her *Narrative of Sojourner Truth*. Sojourner begins speaking out for the abolitionist cause and women's rights.

1851	Sojourner gives her "Ain't I a woman?" address in Akron, Ohio.
1853	Sojourner visits Harriet Beecher Stowe.
1857	Sojourner moves to Michigan.
1863	Stowe publishes "Sojourner Truth, the Libyan Sibyl." Frances D. Gage publishes her account of the "Ain't I a woman?" speech.
1864	Sojourner moves to Washington, D.C., where she meets with President Lincoln and works on behalf of freedmen.
1865	Sojourner sues after being discriminated against and injured by a streetcar conductor.
1870	Sojourner begins calling for the resettlement of freedmen in the western territories.
1875	Sojourner publishes an updated version of her autobiography.
1879	Sojourner travels to Kansas to work with the Exodusters.
1883	Sojourner dies at her home in Battle Creek, Michigan.

GLOSSARY

Amazon In Greek mythology, a member of a nation of female warriors.

ardent Strongly enthusiastic.

charismatic Having the ability to attract others easily, often through personality.

contentious Causing or likely to cause conflict.

cooperative An enterprise or organization owned and managed jointly by those who make use of its facilities or services.

cult Usually any small religious group outside the mainstream and often dismissed as fraudulent.

discrimination The act of judging someone on a basis other than individual merit, such as race.

emancipation The act of freeing from bondage.

feminist One who believes in or works for women's political, economic, and social equality with men.

fervor Intense enthusiasm.

Homestead Act An act passed by Congress in 1862 promising ownership of a 160-acre (65-hectare) tract of public land to a citizen or head of a family who had lived on and farmed the land for five years after the initial claim.

illiterate Unable to read or write.

Quaker A member of the Christian group the Religious Society of Friends, which preaches kindness and nonviolence.

Reconstruction The period (1865–1877) during which the states that had seceded were controlled by the federal government before being readmitted to the Union.

refrain A regularly recurring phrase.

secede To formally withdraw from an organization.

slander A spoken statement of false charges that damages someone's reputation.

Spiritualism A philosophical and religious movement that believes in the possibility of communicating with souls after death.

Underground Railroad A secret network that helped fugitive slaves reach safety in the free states or in the British colony of Canada before the United States abolished slavery.

Universalists A religious group believing in the eventual salvation of all of humanity.

FOR MORE INFORMATION

National Civil Rights Museum

450 Mulberry Street

Memphis, TN 38103

(901) 521-9699

Web site: http://www.civilrightsmuseum.org

e-mail: contact@civilrightsmuseum.org

The National Civil War Museum

One Lincoln Circle at Reservoir Park

P.O. Box 1861

Harrisburg, PA 17105

(866) 258-4729

Web site: http://nationalcivilwarmuseum.org

Web Sites

Due to the changing nature of Internet links, the Rosen Publishing Group, Inc., has developed an online list of Web sites related to the subject of this book. This site is updated regularly. Please use this link to access the list:

http://www.rosenlinks.com/ghds/stai

FOR FURTHER READING

Altman, Linda Jacobs. *Slavery and Abolition in American History*. Berkeley Heights, NJ: Enslow Publishers, Inc., 1999.

Bernard, Catherine. *Sojourner Truth: Abolitionist and Women's Rights Activist*. Berkeley Heights, NJ: Enslow Publishers, Inc., 2001.

Golay, Michael. *The Civil War* (America at War). New York: Facts on File, Inc., 1992.

Rogers, James T. *The Antislavery Movement*. New York: Facts on File, Inc., 1994.

Sagan, Miriam. *Women's Suffrage*. San Diego, CA: Lucent Books, 1995.

Taylor, Kimberley Hayes. *Black Abolitionists and Freedom Fighters*. Minneapolis, MN: Oliver Press, 1996.

BIBLIOGRAPHY

Dudley, William, ed. *American Slavery*. San Diego, CA: Greenhaven Press, 2000.

Mabee, Carleton, with Susan Mabee Newhouse. *Sojourner Truth— Slave, Prophet, Legend*. New York: New York University Press, 1995.

Painter, Nell Irvin, ed. *Narrative of Sojourner Truth*. New York: Penguin Books, 1998.

Painter, Nell Irvin. *Sojourner Truth, a Life, a Symbol*. New York: W. W. Norton and Company, 1996.

Stalcup, Brenda, ed. *Women's Suffrage*. San Diego, CA: Greenhaven Press, 2000.

Stetson, Erlene, and Linda David. *Glorying in Tribulation: The Lifework of Sojourner Truth*. East Lansing, MI: Michigan State University Press, 1994.

PRIMARY SOURCE IMAGE LIST

Page 4 (top): Undated hand-colored illustration of Sojourner Truth. Artist unknown.

Page 8 (top): Hand-colored photograph of household slave and her charge, circa 1855. Housed at the Library of Congress Prints and Photographs Division in Washington, D.C.

Page 8 (bottom): Photograph of a slave family picking cotton near Savannah, Georgia, around 1860. Housed at the New-York Historical Society.

Page 11: Title page of "Minutes of Proceedings of a Convention of Delegates from the Abolition Societies Established in Different Parts of the United States," 1794. Housed at the Library of Congress Rare Book and Special Collections Division in Washington, D.C.

Page 12: *The American Anti-Slavery Almanac for 1843*. Compiled by Lydia Maria Child and published by the American Anti-Slavery Society. Housed at the Library of Congress Rare Book and Special Collections Division in Washington, D.C.

Page 14 (bottom): Photograph of Susan B. Anthony and Elizabeth Cady Stanton, taken by Napoleon Sarony around 1881.

Page 18: *Isabella Among the Flock*, oil painting by Ed Wong-Longda. Courtesy of the Sojourner Truth Institute of Battle Creek, Michigan.

Page 20: *The Prophet* by Benjamin Folger, published by W. Mitchell in New York, 1834.

Page 22 (left): Cover of *Narrative of Sojourner Truth*, 1875. Housed at the Academic Affairs Library at the University of North Carolina at Chapel Hill.

Page 22 (right): Title page of *Narrative of Sojourner Truth*, 1875. Housed at the Sojourner Truth Institute of Battle Creek, Michigan.

Page 23: Photograph of Frederick Douglass among participants at an abolitionist convention in 1850. Taken by Ezra Greenleaf Weld. Housed at the J. Paul Getty Museum in Los Angeles, California.

Page 26: A Sojourner Truth calling card, circa 1864. Part of the Gladstone Collection at the Library of Congress in Washington, D.C.

Page 28 (left): Photograph of Frances Gage, circa 1865. Housed at the Library of Congress Prints and Photographs Division in Washington, D.C.

Page 28 (right): "The Proceedings of the Woman's Rights Convention, held at Akron, Ohio, May 28 and 29, 1850." Published in 1851. Housed at the Library of Congress in Washington, D.C.

Page 31: June 21, 1851, edition of the *Anti-Slavery Bugle*. Courtesy of Woonsocket Harris Public Library in Woonsocket, Rhode Island.

Page 33: Sojourner Truth's signature, dated April 23, 1880. Courtesy of the Archives of the Historical Society of Battle Creek in Michigan.

Page 35: Engraving of Abraham Lincoln presenting the Emancipation Proclamation to his cabinet. Created by Alexander Hay Ritchie, circa 1866, after an original painting by F. B. Carpenter. Housed at the Library of Congress Prints and Photographs Division in Washington, D.C.

Page 37 (left): *Libyan Sibyl*, marble statue, 1861, photographed by Richard T. Nowitz at the Smithsonian Museum of American Art in Washington, D.C.

Page 37 (right): "Sojourner Truth, the Libyan Sibyl," magazine article by Harriet Beecher Stowe, published in the *Atlantic Monthly* in April 1863.

Page 39: February 25, 1864, letter from Sojourner Truth to Mary Gale (dictated to Euphemia Cockrane). Housed at the Library of Congress in Washington, D.C.

Page 41: *Glimpses at the Freedmen—The Freedmen's Union Industrial School, Richmond, Va.*, wood engraving by James E. Taylor, 1866. Housed at the Library of Congress Prints and Photographs Division in Washington, D.C.

Page 43 (bottom): "Ho for Kansas," 1878 poster. Issued by the Real Estate and Homestead Association. Housed at the Library of Congress Prints and Photographs Division in Washington, D.C.

Page 47: Photograph of a painting of Abraham Lincoln and Sojourner Truth, circa 1893. Housed at the Library of Congress Prints and Photographs Division in Washington, D.C.

INDEX

About the Author

Corona Brezina is a freelance writer who lives in Chicago, Illinois.

Photo Credits

Cover, pp. 4, 14 © Bettmann/Corbis; pp. 8 (top), 28 (left), 35, 43, 47 Library of Congress Prints and Photographs Division; p. 8 (bottom) © New-York Historical Society, NY; pp. 11, 12 Library of Congress Rare Book and Special Collections Division; pp. 15, 28 (right), 39 Library of Congress Manuscript Division; p. 18 © Sojourner Truth Institute of Battle Creek; p. 22 (left) © The Academic Affairs Library, the University of North Carolina at Chapel Hill; pp. 22 (right), 33 © courtesy of the Archives of the Historical Society of Battle Creek; p. 23 © The J. Paul Getty Museum; p. 26 Gladestone Collection, Library of Congress; p. 31 courtesy of the Woonsocket Harris Public Library; p. 37 (left) © Richard T. Nowitz/Corbis; p. 37 (right) The *Atlantic Monthly*, April 1863; p. 41 © Corbis; p. 48 Cindy Reiman.

Designer: Les Kanturek; **Editor:** Wayne Anderson